Relationships
The Value there of
By Devine Garrett Sr.

This is not a book of advice but rather a perspective and perception of the way it's seen through the eyes of the author. This book can be used as a tool of encouragement, entertainment or simply supportive tool depending on the individual whom consumes the information and the purpose thereof.

*Through out this book are several random photos inserted for personal enjoyment.

Preface

This originally started off as basic notes and memos that I was writing as a reminder to myself I order to not lose focus and track of my own situations and make sure I keep things clear for myself so that I can navigate through life with out going over the same bumps and pot holes in the road but at some point I realized that their are many people whom have gone through or will go through these same or similar situations and may need to read my perspective and perception of the way is see things on this topic. I hope to provide comfort and support to those in need by providing and sharing my notes. Thanks for reading

Relationships & Influence.

The greatest asset relies upon the relationships that you build and your ability to manage them. The quality of those relationships and the stewardship thereof. In a relationship it must be beneficial for both parties. Knowing or unknowingly both parties must gain something that will enhance their paths of achievement in what ever targeted goal that maybe. Once a relationship becomes one sided that relationship instantly becomes an unhealthy relationship. The foundation of the relationship must be built on positive cornerstones. Honesty, Transparency & Loyalty. Any hidden agendas will eventually show. Depending on the nature of that agenda it may hinder or bring toll on the relationship damaging the relationship in result. Unhealthy habits from past relationships often pass on into new and current relationships which will sabotage those relationships. It tends to eat away at them slowly but surely like a cancer. You must immediately brake all unhealthy yokes and contracts breached. Most relationships take time and consistency. Think of relationship building like buying a house. The longer you keep it the more equity it gains. As long as it's an healthy one.

Watch the company you keep.

Sometimes the people whom you share the most time with aren't the ones you can trust but rather are people whom begin to simply tolerate your actions or vise versa. It's best to take time to analyze your own character and values often in order to make sure its not you that's being the toxic person in any relationship that you have wether it be with a sibling, parent lover or friend. Even co workers may find themselves tolerating your bad behavior not only because they're bonded to you through work but also because they possibly became numb to your actions and have accepted it to be apart of you. Usually what you think of yourself isn't always how others perceive you. I'm not telling you to spend much time worrying about what others think of you but I am encouraging you to take time out to look in the mirror and make sure your personal perception of yourself is realistic and accurate as possible. It's ok to have different belief system and understanding as others but make sure that your standing on the foundation of knowledge so that the manifestation that you get from it will enhance your wisdom and give you and those whom observe your ways the correct understanding of what they are perceiving of you.

Benefits of Relationships

Relationship can bring you prosperity through the resources that one can gather from the many different types one may have. You may be in need of a new source of income and one of your associates may have a side business that they're willing to expose to you or simply know of some one hiring for a position that you would be suitable for or better yet an investment that you're more then ready to invest in. You never know who may be valuable to your livelihood until you start to reach out for those things needed. I encourage you to always study and learn new things and practice and participate in those things that you learn so that you may pick up many skills making you become a very valuable asset to others as well. People always told me the five people you hang around the most is a reflection of ones self, meaning if you're around 5 poor thinking people you'll definitely be the sixth one. If you're around five wealthy minded people you'll become the sixth one. This can be true to an extent but in my case I spend a lot of time alone by myself and the people I have in my circumference the most are my young children and my spouse. They're usually looking to me for guidance not the other way around. So I'm their greatest influence. So I'm usually reading books from authors of great value to me and watching and listening to podcast about a variety of things such as generational wealth, real-estate, Music, entrepreneurship, branding, marketing, healthcare and so on. I make sure that I implicate the things that I learn in my daily life to test the information and make sure that it can be applied and is accurate before I share it with my family and others. If I'm learning something that I haven't yet pursued then I make sure to share my references of where I've gotten the information so that it can be analyzed a judge for ones self. Im very careful not to share toxic nor poisonous information with others. I want to enhance people's lives not destroy them.

Be careful what you consume

Growing up my teachers taught you are what you eat but what a better way to put it would have been you become what you consume. If you put garbage in your body whether it be food, music, information or environment then you'll most likely become affected by those things. Humans usually adapt to their environment so if you're around unethical people with horrible logic and perspectives there's a great chance that you will pick up parts of their ideology for yourself. You'll either build on those beliefs or destroy those beliefs with in but as long as you surround yourself around it long enough it will penetrate into your belief system in some way. We must protect ourselves from the world unshackles of expectations and look with in ourselves and design the life we want for ourselves. There are many ways to do things but you have to find the correct way to do things for you. Do things in such a way that when executing your plans to accomplish your goals it works. You must watch your circle that you keep. Pay close attention to those that encourage you and ones that attempt to discourage you. The negative people in your life must walk the plank. They must exist your life. It's best to be alone or with just few whom inspire and encourage you then to be with many whom keeps creating fictional obstacles to put in your way. Many people project their fears on others because they're scared for what ever reason but those emotions belong entirely to them. Never incorporate someone's else's negative thinking into your plan unless you're in the business of solving other people's problems and then and only then is it ok to hear them out from their perspective so that you may analyze and explore the solutions. Showing others how you want to be treated is illustrated through how you carry and treat yourself. Remember your legacy is everything. How people remember you when your gone has more significant value than money itself. You must conduct yourself in such a way that leaves a positive impression. Take the time out to build a foundation based on righteous principles.

Self Care

Always remember to build a relationship with yourself as well. If you don't truly know yourself, then how can you truly know how to treat others. You should always practice self care. Make sure you're mental as well as your physical health is ok. Exercise not only helps the physical but also the mental. When exercising you have an opportunity to focus on your thoughts in an amplified way as they cross your mind. You also get the benefits of having good physical health. Being over weight is tied to depression and heart disease. Reading is also very healthy for your personal enhancement. It helps a person relax as well as gain knowledge. It can also assist a person in their thought process of practicing how to compute information even if it's fiction that you're reading. Many people have also found that keeping a journal about their daily experiences and short and long term goals also helps them to keep track of their thoughts as well be able to analyze the things in their life that's beneficial to them. No need to continue to keep the bad habits or do things that's counter productive. Life's too short for those things. Once you truly understand why you operate a certain way it's easier to fathom why someone else may do or desire to do things they do or even conduct themselves in such a manner. The human mind is very intriguing and every element of its function can play a significant part it one's outcome. Self appreciation is important. You must celebrate your accomplishments and progress. From the little things to the big ones. A basic example is if you decide that you need to loose 5 pounds and you apply yourself consistently. Once you reach that goal it's very important to smile and show your self appreciation but make sure you never celebrate in a counter productive way. Don't go binge eat after you achieve your goal. If you decide you want to start a new businesses or learn something new and you achieve that goal, it's also worth the celebration. The things that make you a stronger more established individual is always worth the self praise but be careful not illustrate in too much vanity or it can become a little vain. There's absolutely nothing wrong with being proud of yourself though.

  Once you learn what self love looks like it's easier to identify when others love you or even observe yourself falling in love with some one else. Love is the highest elevation of understanding and doesn't always have to be verbally stated but always illustrated. Love can come in a form of communication and concern such as someone making sure you've eaten today or making sure you have a coat and umbrella in the rain so that you don't catch a cold. Sometimes a person might identify that you've had a rough day and simply allow you to talk about it with them. Not necessarily offering advice but rather a shoulder to cry on or lend an ear. People often need help and it's not always do it for me but rather do it with me which is often the comfort of encouragement needed to get through. Love is having patience and a since of tolerance to an extent giving a person or self time to grow and make a change. You must also tell a person the truth even if it hurts. Once you tell a person the truth you must give them a certain amount of time to make those changes resulting in you tolerating the flaw or incompetence until the grow or solve the issue. Just make sure that it's not a situation where you're compromising your own self love or safety. You must always think ten steps ahead I order to protect yourself and those that not only you love but also those whom love you. Never allow a relationship you have with someone that you love put those whom love you in danger. Some one whom truly loves you would never ask you to sacrifice your well being for their self purposes. A basic example is if someone puts their selves in a bad situation such as domestic violence wouldn't ask you to go an risk your freedom to solve their problem knowing that the put their selves in that situation and it could result in you being killed or going to jail over something they have the power to solve themselves by simply cutting ties or walking away from the relationship. In many cases even getting the proper authorities involved. Having you do it is like a King or Queen rather pushing a pond. Never become someone's pond. This is your life and you must protect it in every way possible because you only get one life.

Know when enough is enough

Never stay in a one sided relationship. It takes both parties in order to make any healthy relationship work. I personally been with my spouse for over 20years and I must admit it's something that takes work everyday. Either you're sacrificing or your compromising in order to make sure both parties needs are met. Any time you feel stressed or overwhelmed by any relationship and you address it with that person, if your concerns are down played or not took seriously then it's definitely time to reevaluate your relationship. Mental or Physical abuse is never ok.

Know how to differentiate the difference in relationships, some people aren't your friends but rather an associate and they need to be treated as such. Never give some one the keys to your heart if you don't have the keys to theirs. Never give people too much attention unless you find them as a threat and in that case it's chess not checkers and you need to get and stay away from them. Yes, an exception can be given to children. Children need and deserve your attention. They're still being molded into adults and love is an action word not just a simply phrase to be thrown around carelessly. Although baby do it. Words a very deceiving. Pay close attention to the actions not just the words. Words are only to back up the actions. If they are not in alignment then that persons word can't be considered as bond therefore they shouldn't be full trusted. Trust people's patterns more than their words. People tend to create habits that's hard to break but words are typically thrown around freely. Some people words are meaningless. Co workers are co workers not your friends. At the moment you no longer work with them your yoke is broken. Family a lot of time take at vantage of being family and will abuse a relationship when it comes to business so I usually try not to mix the two. Business partners can become close as family but know the terms are built on business. Families terms are built on business and rarely cross over due to anytime business goes wrong they almost always result back to "Hey we're family!" Business has no heart! Remember what is a relationship if you can't relate and what's the point of a ship if it doesn't go anywhere. At the moment you find yourself in a relationship that serves neither party any service then you no longer need that relationship. Relationships are like plants you must give it nourishment, sunlight and water. Think if you have a spouse that's scared to be seen with you in the public then is that really your spouse? If your spouse never gives you any attention or spend time with you then that's like a plant not getting any nourishment. Without nourishment relationships grow weak. Communication and quality time gives it strength. The more distance between someone the easier it becomes to do without that person. People play positions and if you don't play your position in a relationship then your position will become up for grabs. The person being deprived will search for a replacement. Consciously or unconsciously people seek to have their needs met. Make sure to make the best of your time. Like I said before sometimes you can waist a lot of valuable time spending it with the wrong people and often not even realize it. Some people are so fun to be with but have bad values. Some people characters are awful but know how to have a good time. Usually those are the finesse artists. They know how to get what they want out of you and leave you with nothing but an empty bank account.

Be careful for nothing

Watch out for wording and labeling of relationships. People often try to say you're my brother, cousin, sister, friend, family ex..but ignore those words. Words can be very deceiving but rather watch very closely to their actions. If their words aren't in alignment with their actions then what's the true value in the relationship. The relationships value is as sacred as its foundation. Therefore always look listen and observe. The reality of its truth will reveal itself always. If a person isn't sincere there are always signs that may show you. For an example, if a person acts one way towards you and then some one that they're more acquainted with walks into the circle and they begin to treat you differently that's a flag. If a person makes a promise to you and they are always known to follow through but for some reason once some one else gets involved with the project or situation the person becomes very hesitant to follow through. There are many examples that I can illustrate but it truly becomes to each is own do to every situation is different and so are the elements and methods of operation. It's up to you to pay very close attention to each situation very closely.

Watch the energy that you put out.

Make sure to carry yourself with the upmost respect for yourself and others. That's the only way to assure you can demand others to respect you. People often treat you by the obvious standards that they see you hold yourself to. So if you don't take pride in loving yourself don't expect others to illustrate love toward you. Your passions and dreams, the things that appear to make you tick will drive the aura around you that will non verbally express to others how you expect to be treated. I recall growing up as a child I yarned for love and attention but didn't have the appropriate communication skills to get it. I was very impressionable and thought other's opinions mattered. I often found myself acting like a tough guy getting into fights with bullies for picking on people I wanted to be friends with not realizing the exact people I was protecting would begin to fear me thinking I was the bully of the bullies. The ones I ended up making friends with over time was the actual bullies. I found myself trying to defend a reputation instead of building character. It wasn't until many lonely nights in a jail cell and them lonely nights homeless with no where to go that I begin to see the reality of it all. You must show love in order to receive love and the love and energy you put out must be healthy otherwise you'll get jealousy and envy disguised as friendships. Some even will compete with you for the shine. Be very careful of the company you keep. Make sure you're around those with similar goals so that you don't have to trust what they say but what the do instead. Actions are just as important as the words that come before them.

Relationships Fade as interest Change

    Sometimes simply people out grow each other. It doesn't have to be a particular reason why someone no longer wants to be with are around another, sometimes people simply grow in to different directions resulting in loosing interest in being in each others presence. Make sure someone else's acceptance of approval is never attached to your own self confidence or ability to show up for your own goals and accomplishments. Remember you are created for the purpose that you were created and they are created for the purposes they was created. No one human are born with the same finger print therefore their purpose and desires here on earth is allowed to be different. Their options and opinions are allow to be different than yours. You must simply stay focused and encouraged to achieve your own goals. No one can tell you different. Sometimes the universe will allow everyone to walk away from you so that you will find your purpose. It's not always something wrong with you nor them, just a moment of self truth must occasionally occur in order to reveal itself to you so that you may know whom you truly are. Sometimes you think you're thinking for self but I'm reality your program by other's opinions. Not just your circle of people you deal with daily but also the music you listen to and the broadcast you watch whether it be television, internet or social media.

Once you detach yourself you will be able to find yourself and think for yourself. Those things should only be used as a tool such as research or entertainment, not personal influence. Knowing that people can be easily influenced by those things they become a very good marketing tool. It definitely enhances your brand awareness. People have problems and if you provide a solution for those problems you can easily build a relationship around that. There are many types of relationships or interactions that take place. Make sure they're healthy and not one sided. Growth is always needed in order to strengthen those relationships. If you never communicate with those people frequently don't be embarrassed when they forget whom you are and what services or product you provide.

Always remember the initial reason why and how you first encountered a person or company. Never cross that boundary and if by chance you do remind yourself the foundation of thereof. If it's business then keep it business, if it's pleasure then stick to the pleasure but rarely can you cross over successfully without weakening the foundation. Never do business with family if possible because they usually take advantage of situations using the label Family as leverage to keep things in their favor. Never bring people you do business with home or put them in your personal life because they will keep that in mind in order to have leverage for their personal gain. Keep the lines and never cross them. Over time it's real easy to get relaxed but that can play out badly. Stay aware and never loose sight.

Legacy

One of the most important things to think about is that when you leave this earth what will your legacy be? No one will care about how many hours you work, how much your salary was our even how busy you was but they will remember how you made them feel, what you taught them and what you stood for. They will remember was your word bond and could they always count on you. They will remember the moments that you made them feel special or even made them smile. They will remember if you was an hater or congratulatory. They will remember was your serous person or full of jokes. Those are the things that truly count, not your bank account. Spend as much time with those that you love and care about because when it's over it's absolutely over. No second chances to get it right. We only get one go at it. We must make it count. We must remember that life isn't only about us and our experiences but also others and how we affect theirs. Everyone must take full responsibility for their own actions and simply admit when they're wrong. No excuses. Sometimes you might try to do good and it may back fire learn to forgive yourself and move on. Things happen.

Money Relationship

So I've talked a little about many types of relationships but one I haven't briefly spoke on was your relationship with finances. How do you look at your income? Do you look at it as your friend or enemy? Money is a token of exchange that represents a value. It's generated by providing a service or product. Once it becomes consistent it becomes a stream of income which can be used as a tool to either consume items or create leverage to acquire assets. Assets are things that create streams of income such as businesses or property where you're the owner which can result in you having more revenue generated on a consistent basis. Money is definitely a good thing to have but your perception of it has to be clear in order for the relationship to be healthy. If you get money and you spend it on liabilities only then you'll rarely have any which would make you struggle to get more of it but if you get money and invest in it then you'll always have it and with the right investments you'll obtain it more abundantly. Money makes money. Money likes to be invited into situations where it can grow and become more. Money comes to those whom makes those situations possible. Money leaves those whom spends it making it deplete itself. When the book states "The love of money is the root of evil" it's actually referring to the spirit one possess inside their selves to obtain it. When you have a healthy relationship with money it can become an excellent tool to draw love near instead of distributing hatred in order to get it. A lot of times ethics plays apart in this. If you generate your stream of income from bad ethos then you most definitely will find yourself being possessed with an unhealthy spirit which will encourage you to do evil things to obtain money. To have healthy ethics and a righteous code of conduct will in return create many positive opportunities and chances for you to create and generate multiple sources of income in abundance. Always set a goal and know the steps that it takes to get there. Never skip the steps or you'll find yourself back tracking. The foundation must be solid and built on good principles. If you want things to prosper then pay close attention and analyze things as you go. Once you accomplish your goal make sure to pay it forward meaning reach back and teach some one else the steps from your experience in hopes that they may be able to have such the success that you're experiencing. In doing so that alone is also a way to generate another income. People always are willing to purchase classes, tutorials or materials on how to do something. Just take not that how you start a relationship is usually how you keep the relationship. Let me explain. If you meet a person and what attracts them to you is your accomplishments and you begin to teach them how to obtain that same goal then that relationship is based on you being an outlet of knowledge for them to create an opportunity for them to achieve their goal. At the moment they have completed the lesson your relationship may quickly de solve but if you continue to accomplish new goals of their interest and keep offering them knew information then they become a returning recipient of that information and will continue to feed off of the knowledge that you provide. You never have to be insecure as if you're going to loose a student if your goal is to genuinely help and not control or deceive someone for personal gain.

Lust and Obsession

Sometimes you meet people and you realize that your expectations are entirely too much. One example is you might meet a person that you're sexually attracted to and that person may or may not be attracted to you as well. You and that person begin to have encounters in that nature with each other but the other person only wants that no more. You find your self fantasizing about creating a future with that person with intentions of creating a family and growing old with that person but in reality the foundation of that relationship was based on mere lust. You never take the time out to truly know the good and bad about that person. As the elders would say, you can't see the forest for the trees. Some times you become blinded by the obsession of obtaining what you desire instead of being realistic of what you're actually capable of receiving. I found if you show signs of obsession with some one you get either of the two results, you either get used and abused creating the feeling of you being played when in reality you played yourself or you get the other outcome which is you run a person off. This also happens not in just relationships of the sexual nature but also in business. You can't desire to have some work done by a company so bad not really taking the time out to check their qualifications and past history that they totally play you for your time and milk you for your dime. You must always take time to make your self clear and do the research. Make sure your communication with the other entity is totally understood and they know exactly what your expectations and intentions are otherwise it's your fault if you fall short of getting the results you're reaching for. Think about yourself and your own personality. If a potential client wants you to do something and you keep telling them that's outside of your range of expertise and they ignore you and keep instruct you so the job what would you do? Either you're most likely to take their money and do the best you can. Maybe you may even over charge them and outsource the work to a third party and take the credit for as if your company did it or you would simply cut all dialogue and avoid the client blaming it on bad communication. Always research. Make sure you know the history of the person or entity and the qualifications. Make sure you yourself know exactly what your goal is that you wish to achieve and if they meet that criteria. Once in doing so and only after doing so you may begin to have a clear over standing with the other party making sure the relationship will be healthy. Otherwise you're setting yourself up for failure.

Exploiting

In some situations one may be naive to the fact that they're being exploited by an individual that they put their loyalty or trust in. Exploitation comes in many different forms but the basic way to explain it is when a person is being used for someone else's selfish gain at what ever expense. Sometimes people find theirselves being exploited by their own parents, family or friends. You have to always think about what you personally have to loose and gain in every situation. Never put some one else's dreams ,fantasies or goals before your own at the risk of you loosing something as important as your freedom or maybe worst your life. You can love a person or care for a person so much that you're willing to put it all on the line but you truly need to sit back and think not only would this person do it for you but also can you live with this decision. Look at the final outcome before stepping into the situation that can occur. Not only would it be appreciated but also what gratification would you personally get out of it. Are you that desperate to show some one that you're here to support them even if it means leaving this earth or being incarcerated, not even being able to bask in their victory? Are you willing to compromise your total existence in order to please someone else? If so then that person better be your minor child and you're doing it in order to provide them with a prosperous future in some way otherwise I find it to be game goofy and naive of you in a dramatic way. There's no one, entity or organization that you should love more then you love yourself. If so then that relationship most definitely can't be a healthy one. A lot of people do things to fit in and be accepted but if I'm doing so you have to compromise whom you are and what you truly believe in, compromise your principles and morels that you stand for then honestly what's the true value of that acceptance? You should be accepted for whom you truly are even if it means being different than the common individual that they are use to. Think about what they're asking you to do. Why are they pacifically asking you? Why can't they do it themselves? Is it a life changing event? There are many factors to pay close attention to. What's the cost! Whom will actually benefit? What would your gratification be and how would they show you their gratitude?if these are questions you can't answer them you must move on. Someone whom truly cares would never ask you to make such sacrifices knowing that it's going to jeopardize you and something of significant value to you for their own self gain. Remember to keep all relationships healthy. No one is worth you not being able to Ben your true self.

Depreciating Value

Did you know that some relationships naturally dissolve? Not because they don't have anything in common so to speak but rather because the eventually stop bringing each other significant value. Example is that one friend or relative that you use to be accompanied with every day and now you look up and realize y'all haven't been around each other in years for what ever reason. At one point they was apart of your daily dealings but now they're association with you have become very distant. It's not as if you have lost love for them but you no longer nurture the relationship. You no longer call them to stay informed on how y'all can't share value. You no longer see them on a consistent enough basis where they can see how to assist you where and when you need assistance. Yes, it goes both ways but the relationship is no longer an important substance in your life. That relationship is depreciating and eventually will de solve so little until it won't exist. It doesn't have to only be for associating with people direct it can also count for your favorite programming whether it be a t.v.show, magazine or social media platform.

Once you stop feeding it attention you start to no longer crave its subsistence which use to give you value. At some point you do away with it altogether and begins to have no existential value in your reality.

Down play

Never keep relationships with people or entities that try to down play your

concerns or services in order to make theirs or themselves seem superior to others. Usually that's a sign of jealousy, insecurity and in some cases flat out hating. People feel called out sometimes when they're put in a position to illustrate or demonstrate a skill or talent that they're left efficient in. Sometimes to downplay others can make them think that they took the attention off of themselves and put the focus momentarily on someone else in reality when a potential client or person ask you for your services or product it's usually because they're interested in you particularly and what it is that you can do or provide but if you blow them off or direct the attention away from you then you take the tension off of you. Notice haters can come in many forms or fashions. Haters can be your family members, fake friends or even business partners. If you ever find yourself feeling as if you're being competed with by your own team mate then you must sit back and reassess the situation and relationship. No one needs a wants to be accompanied by a Judas, unless you plan to use them against their selves. Let me explain. Sometimes if you know that some one isn't loyal then you can often put them in position to be around some one on purpose that you know they will sale you out to. In doing so you will gain power over the situation because you actually made a well thought out chess move. Always think things thoroughly. Make a plan A through Z. Stay 50 steps ahead at all times. Just like the weather conditions can always change. Never allow someone else's negativity drive you to making revenge your main agenda and goal. Financial freedom and inner peace is always a better goal to spend your energy on achieving than trying to get even. If you're not born with malice in your heart naturally but they are then you will loose every time trying to beat them at their own game. There's an old saying "it's in you not on you!" If you got the gift you got it but if you don't then it's a skill and you have to practice with great repetition in order to master it. When a person is born evil or envious they need little practice because it's natural to them. They best way to win anything against a hater is by succeeding. Success is always the key.

Conclusion

Thank you for taking the moment out to read what some may call my memoirs or basic life notes on the many different types of relationships and my perspective or perception there of. I truly hope this has been a productive read and either enhances your knowledge or gives you basic enlightenment on how others outside of yourself thinks. Please feel free to quote me and share this publication with others. Talk about it on social media and refer others to this. Much love and prosperity to you in abundance always. Have a glorious prosperous life in abundance always. Peace!

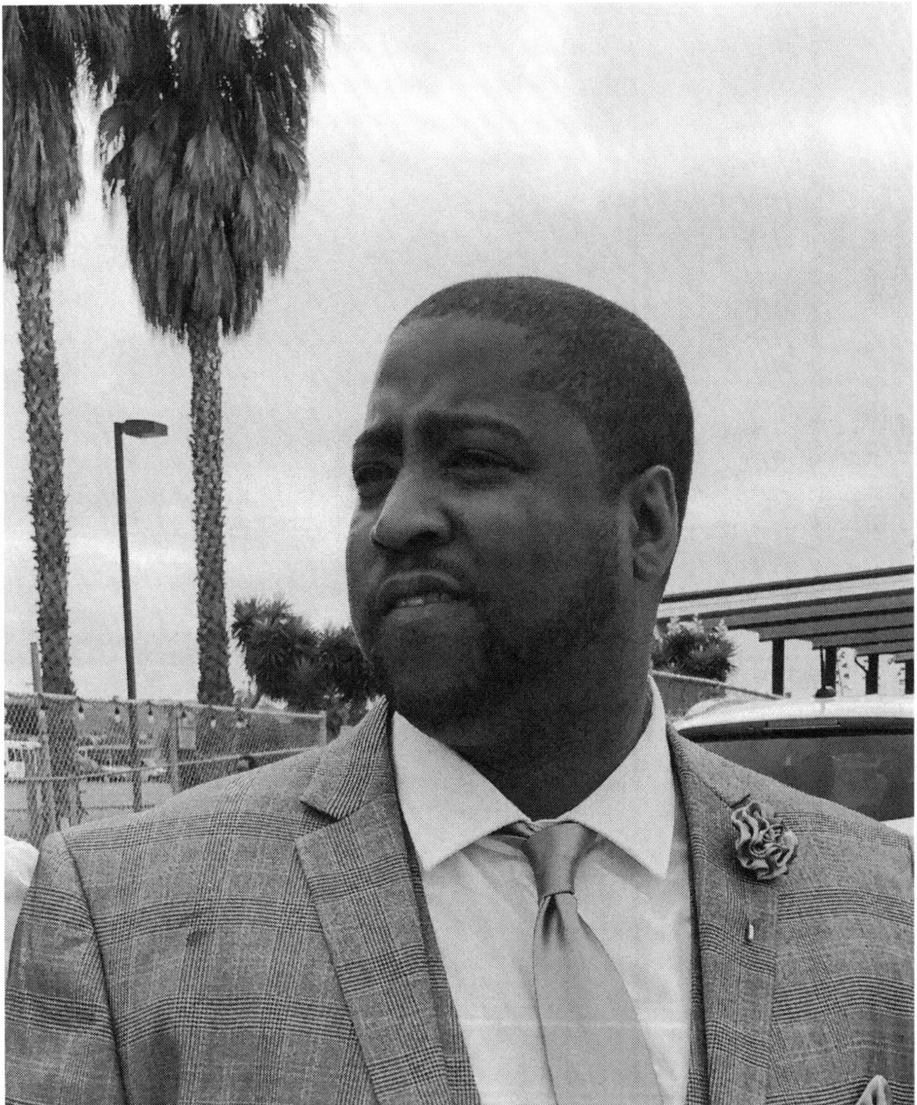

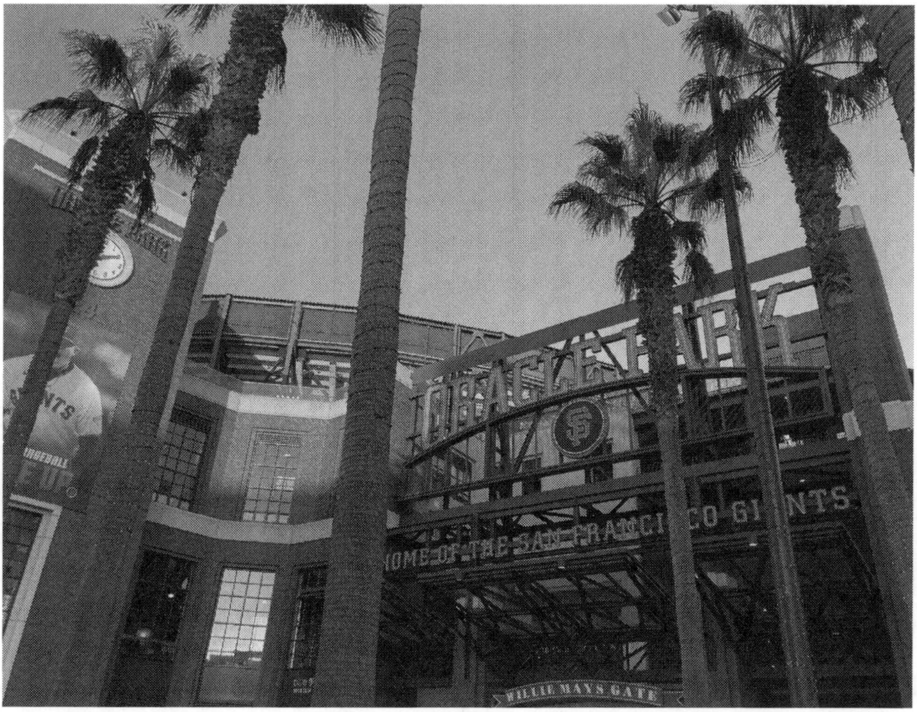
WILLIE MAYS GATE

Made in the USA
Columbia, SC
08 June 2023